WITHDRAWN

The Cedar Canoe

The Cedar Canoe

Poems by Karen Fish

The University of Georgia Press
Athens and London

© 1987 by Karen Fish
Published by the University of Georgia Press
Athens, Georgia 30602
All rights reserved

Designed by Betty P. McDaniel
Set in Berkeley Old Style Book
The paper in this book meets the guidelines for
permanence and durability of the Committee on
Production Guidelines for Book Longevity of the
Council on Library Resources.

Printed in the United States of America

91 90 89 88 87   5 4 3 2 1

Library of Congress Cataloging in Publication Data

Fish, Karen, 1959–
  The cedar canoe.
    I. Title.
PS3556.I77C4 1987   811'.54   87-13755
ISBN 0-8203-0968-0 (alk. paper)
ISBN 0-8203-0969-9 (pbk.: alk. paper)

British Library Cataloging in Publication
Data available

with gratitude and love
  Janice Marion Cooper

Acknowledgments

The author and publisher gratefully acknowledge the following publications where these poems first appeared.

American Poetry Review: "Jeanne d'Arc," "The Cedar Canoe," "Black Ice," "The Awakening," "Equivalent"
Antioch Review: "The Ferry: Woods Hole," "Venice, Widow in a Gondola 1891," "The Orchard," "Self-Portrait with a Camellia Branch"
Crazyhorse: "Sunday Morning," "Signs of Life"
Denver Quarterly: "The Viaduct"
Florida Review: "Florida"
Ironwood: "The Prayer"
Kalliope: "Translation"
Michigan Quarterly: "Dusk"
Missouri Review: "Catherine of Aragon"
New Yorker: "The Lake," "Approximation"
North American Review: "The Good Return"
Shankpainter: "Late August"
Yale Review: "Wishbone"

I would like to thank the Fine Arts Work Center in Provincetown and the Humanities Center of Loyola College in Maryland for their generous support that allowed me to complete this book. I also want to extend special thanks to Stephen Berg, Arthur Byron, and David St. John for their constant encouragement.

The Simone Weil quotes are from *The Simone Weil Reader: A Legendary Spiritual Odyssey of Our Time,* edited by George A. Panichas (New York: David McKay Company, 1977). The quotes contained in "Dusk" are from *The Mapmakers: The Story of the Great Pioneers in Cartography from Antiquity to the Space Age,* by John Noble Wilford (New York: Vintage Books, 1982). "Self-Portrait with a Camellia Branch" was inspired by Gillian Perry's *Paula Modersohn-Becker* (New York: Harper and Row, 1979). Lines 11–12 and 15–17 of "Black Ice" are from *diane arbus* (Aperture Monograph, Millerton, N.Y., 1972).

Contents

One

Approximation   3
Dusk   4
Black Ice   6
Orbiting the Sun   8
The White Shed   9
The Orchard   11
Florida   13
Signs of Life   14
The Ferry: Woods Hole   16

Two

Jeanne d'Arc   19
Wishbone   21
Catherine of Aragon   23
The Good Return   25
Venice, Widow in a Gondola 1891   27
Safe House: Brandon, Vermont   28
Self-Portrait with a Camellia Branch   30
The Prayer   32
The Viaduct   33

Three

My Father   37
Late August   38
Equivalent   39
Translation   41
The Cedar Canoe   42

Sunday Morning   43
Crossing   45
The Awakening   47
The Lake   48

*It is when one is in extreme thirst,
ill with thirst; then one no longer thinks of the act
of drinking in relation to oneself, or even the act of drinking
in a general way. One merely thinks of water,
actual water itself, but the image of water is like a cry
from our whole being.*

—Simone Weil

One

Approximation

The sun is slow, its light tugging across the fields
like someone learning magic, pulling a white tablecloth
out from under old silver place settings for the first time.
Or I think of gray-haired men swimming naked,
drifting across the Roman bathtub—talking through the steam.
The shadows attached to the gestured trees are long and slender,
like the fingers of a woman playing piano.

The other day after you left,
I washed the dishes, drank like an Indian
who drinks the white man's whiskey,
and walked into the rain.

The dirt road that runs down the hill
behind the small country church became a muddy stream,
and the dilapidated red barn looked more and more
like a monarch
sitting on the highest point of land.
I walked down the thin shoelace of road,
the one the tractor takes between the fields,
and thought of the black-and-white photograph of the women,
German civilians, leaving their blasted farmhouse,
1945—the smoke rising like mist.

Dusk

in memory, for my father Charlie (1929–1976)

This is the world of the grainy photograph, the dots
just a quick semblance of leaves. The distant trees appear
pushed back, foggy, all details lost for lack of light.
Leaves become tones of green, white—
the particulars just patches, patches of color, blunt
as a brushstroke, just the idea put down,
the suggestion, the shape of things.

The far away firing range is silent
and I am standing in high grass in a clearing. The grain
is still green. I am suddenly stopped,
looking backward,

the thing that arrests me is how . . .
the deer come down from the forested hills with the onset
of night and sift with the darkness through rows of corn.
The road is white, a perfume of snow—
dropped blossoms cover the gravel.

And the mind is trained from early childhood to forget,
to veil what is too painful to recall.
This is the mind, the cross-stitch, a few strands of thread,
the work of nimble fingers. This field tight as needlepoint.

The heart is a map, a landscape.
I think of history, hear my teacher's voice—
the list of animals that migrate, the huge map crisscrossed—

latitude, longitude, elk, whale

the continents looked like misshapen pancakes
floating on the surface of the skillet.
And we did walk through the huge heart, the museum of love,
up the right ventricle, a circular staircase, and down
through the pounding hall, the left ventricle—
out into the noonday sun of Philadelphia.

I am little and imagining myself back in time—
The teacher stands in front of the map
and as she talks, she moves the lit wand,
for the entirety of the sixteenth century,
maps of New England consisted of a single line separating ocean
from land, accompanied by a string of place-names to indicate
landmarks along the shore;
the interior remained blank . . .

blank as deep forests, woods, dark—looming ahead
like adulthood, like experience, just a suggestion.

I think of you as if you were simply on the other side
of this continent; in the distance the moon is a peach color
and rises above the margin of hills, a peach moon between
the twisted static trees—
this is the astonishing and unadorned landscape.

The mind is trained from childhood to forget,
to veil what is painful—
the heart is a landscape larger than the palm
of a hand.
Suddenly, I have returned intact, and recognizing
your face, in my face, I whisper—

come back.

Black Ice

In a single night
cold air from Canada swings across the lake.
It freezes quickly, no air bubbles, no ripples,
one sheet of unreflecting ice.
Black ice.

The trees along the edge of the lake
rise up like chimneys of smoke.
The skaters pause as they step
onto the ice.

A woman says,
"the thing that's important to know is that you never know.
You are always sort of feeling your way."
She is a photographer, she is taking our picture,
and we are smiling and holding our skates.
"Lately, I've been struck with how I really love
what I can't see in a photograph. An actual physical darkness.
It's very thrilling for me to see darkness again."

I skate off alone, around the small islands.
The sky is stuffed with snow. Soon, I will stop
imagining how cold the water is, the way my foot
could shatter through the ice as if I were kicking in
a glass pane in a door.

I think about my cane chair, how effortless
it gave in to my weight as my foot slipped through.
A blind woman recanes the chair. She tells me,

"I can feel the rasp of dried grass slide between my fingers
but I can't see the pattern."

Then, I think of words
and how I could tell this over and over.

There are old men in the distance
laughing white breaths
driving stakes into the ground for the snow fences.

Orbiting the Sun

for June

Once again the ground thaws under the sun's hot thumb.
The constants all reappear like children at a bus stop
year after year: hawks circling the pasture stream,
the geese assembling
over the cornfield, going north,
their barking falling around us like rain.

This is the season of deception,
our clothes no longer cased in ice on the line.
We know now what will follow, the stream's overflow—
swelling with what it cannot physically contain.
The ground that slowly drinks with its tense impatient desire
and wants to start again.

We are like this.

Ahead are only the long evenings of summer,
the lush resprouting, the green shoots poking
their illustrious heads up through the still water
of the pond.

The White Shed

for my mother

> Outside the heart there is only the wound of time.
> —Jean Joubert

The cratered moon was in focus
and out in the afternoon sky.
The shed sat like a huge bee box at the end of the lawn.
I used to get locked in there
by the neighborhood boys—
while laughing hard all the strength would drain
from my body like water absorbed in sand.
The boys would pile their short, thin bodies
against the outside of the ill-fitting door,
with me laughing collapsed against the splinter of light
at the hinge.

Inside were the mud-stiffened fingers
of my mother's gardening gloves, the smell of chemicals
for rose bushes, the peat moss bag half full and folded over,
unused seed packets, two bales of hay for extended sitting
and the groundhog hole—the dirt, fresh and loose under the
    overturned chaise lounge.
There was also a wasp's nest hanging like a piñata
where the black wall and ceiling met.
A gray papier mâché mask.

The darkness in that shed was the darkness of deep water.
The college chapel bells were rolling over
in the evening at the end of summer, rolling
like huge barrels down the street.
That is when, finally,

a wasp traveled—
crawled up underneath my pant leg.

My mother was in the back field
for that one evening out of the year when
she took the scythe and cut down the long grass—
in the fog of gnats and conspiring of far-off music.
It was as if there was music,
the way the sunlight hung behind her head.

The Orchard

If it were the beginning of the day
the sun would be fingering its way through the branches.
But it is dusk, and I am alone
sitting on my jacket on the incline of a rut
which separates the fruit trees.

Gnats confuse themselves around my head
like the things I don't want to remember.
I used to bring lovers here;
we would park on the road,
and walk
into the orchard—touching each other in the tough
dried grass which poked through the cover
to the whine of a chainsaw way off.

Water flushes a stone springhouse:
a biplane practices in the air as the birds
slowly quiet.
I wonder about the moon—
is tonight the night, or tomorrow, that it will be full
and roll like a coin across the sky?

I remember the stories, my mother's voice
over the bathtub as she scrubbed the white soap
into the blue washcloth, grabbing my small foot.
Beauty and the Beast.
    Thumbelina,
floating in a leaf cup
taken by the current, spinning, surrounded by white petals—

She is so small nothing is beyond her. She can do anything.
Illusion is everything.

It is hard to imagine the apples now.
The buds are green and tight.
I think of the red-black hand of branches,
row after row playing dead like the dog—
Appearance is everything.

The illusion of not-waiting.

It can be learned.
The blossoms fall from the anxious green knot
that will later be the fruit
in the early summer air
which is cool like a precious metal.

Florida

The nights down south are over:
the way his thumb would catch the screen-door lock
on his trips out, and his cigarette would sail the length
of the driveway.
Knowing he had other women I drank
and evening slid off the roof like slate shingles.

I would wander off to the shack behind the house,
to my kitchen of chemicals
to bring landscapes up in pans. The house squatting there
in the dark, the radio chattering through gunked screens.
While neighborhood children rode
their bicycles into circles
and took braids from each other's hair.

I can still see his face
wavering on the other side of the grill,
distorted in the waves of heat, and behind him—
secured in the damp shadows of the house,
tense cacti, air plants perched like nests in trees,
everything overgrown—
the quick blur of lizards across the porch . . .
and the spring wasp dragging its legs,
flying low over everything.

Signs of Life

> *she felt free—but there was nothing*
> *she could do about it*
> —Peter Handke

Not knowing he is being watched
your husband counts the splinters in his hands,
walking out to the rim of distance,
toward the barks of dogs. He takes out the telescope
and stands near the barn beside the dead cars for hours.

Within the bleached farmhouse you undress,
your skin tightens and shrinks with the cold as all my spotlights
flood you.
Your skin turns from almond paste to alabaster.

The wallpaper shifts in this light
and the hours slip down the uncarpeted stairs
holding their broken bones in place.
I bring out my camera and take frame after frame;
the ridge of a hill
and the lid of an eye
are the same coming over the land mass . . .

And this is what I think of again and again.
You move, you change,
your face becomes thirty-six different women.

Your breasts and thighs remain faithful
and indifferent,
restful and indifferent. Beyond this

there are only the few stars that throb,
the cornstalks jack-knifed
in the early morning snowfall.

The Ferry: Woods Hole

Small waves smack against
the dock pilings. This is the last run to the islands.
We sit on the bow in wet deck chairs, waiting
for the last horn, watching the cooks in the restaurant
on the dock laugh in the yellow doorway while passing
a cigarette.

I think back to this afternoon,
how under the stiff breeze the seagulls followed the ferry,
shrieking, diving for the bread tossed from the hands
of camera-strapped tourists.

Time floats on, ripped jellyfish.
Last summer the large basket on the back porch
was filled with peaches, and I ate one every evening
after the birds had all flown
to the one tree in the distance.
Then, the children would hunt for slugs in the garden
following the silver trails—a pie pan filled with beer,
a handful of salt.

The ferry will move out, steadily
into the dark water, around the sandbars studded with tall grass
out into the wind and, from where we sit,
we will be anxious, breathless, passing the small party boats
which bob in the harbor—some are capsized from last winter,
and their dark hulls moan like small whales caught in the inlet.

Two

Jeanne d'Arc
May 1431

   for Peter Fish

The men arrived at dusk
with torches to burn the webs from the trees.
The well water had gone bad. And I could smell
the bestial floor as the withered hay began
furiously molting.

And when all the lights had collapsed
with the bruise color of morning, from the next field
the smoke from damp grasses reached me.
It is here I have slept wet-haired on stone.

Some of the women had gone down
into the potato cellars to hide, to breathe
the wet air, to forget the ash that has already
been smeared on their foreheads.

Peasants like rain-worn stones look on, their grief-stunned
faces stare. Early
I had smelled a certain knowledge.
When I heard Your voice the leaves were blowing over
showing their undersides,
the white that so often means rain.

As the priests turn me into fire,
I will say Your name three times.
Then from my breast they will say
they saw a white dove fly.

I am a fir in the gray forest,
farther than my eye can see are the guards in their clatter.

I am a fir in the gray forest dreaming
of ash, the ash beyond the common day
aching again to be green as You,

immutable, seen.

Wishbone

Liverpool 1906

for Emmy

Early evening, while the whole harbor
is a dismal reflection on the water
surrounding the boats—
the masts' dark lace
floating on the tide like collapsed spider webs,

there is a young girl
imagining the horses going to the start,
the cool eyes of the jockeys, the top hats
of the spectators, or a dirigible zig-zagging
above the fields and hedges outside the town.
Her mind moves quickly as a cat
through the holes and openings of fences
and walls of the back alleys while her feet
keep an even time, the sound of her footsteps
ahead of her.

She imagines the electrical wires tangled
around the masts after a storm—
the pulse of words in the telegraph wires
or young rich girls lying on a carpet
with their mother's jewels splattered across
the floor like jacks, like sunlight.

In a minute she is in the door
and has fingered the wishbone from the steaming
white breast of the chicken placed on the wood table.
Her mother stands with mitts still covering her hands.
The girl is collecting wishbones, hanging them on

the nails around her window.
And so, this is what she picks clean first,
sucking the meat away from the thin bones;
it was hers to claim, never to break.

Catherine of Aragon
January 1536

It was cold in the room. Remember the first night,
my plain linen bedgown, the way your fingers grazed
my shoulders, shaking, brushing my red hair away
as the dress dropped to the floor?
Your breath caught in your throat. And my breasts
tightened under your stare.
I was your first, Queen.

You told me that my hair framed my face
the way scrollwork lights the pages of your chronicles,
glinting like gold coin in your palm.

Exiled, to a wet thatched cottage, I wait
for a servant to poke the fire, bring me hissing gossip.
I stand in front of this window, staring out
at the lip of light which separates hill from sky—

I miss you like the taste of water from a silver cup.

Now, you watch Anne, I drop
to my knees, my ladies-in-waiting avoid my eyes.
May she bear you dead sons,
and daughters who cannot know the love of a man.

The keepers of this house will not let
my remains sit long. When they open my breast,
they will find my heart entirely black.
They will cup it in their hands like a small starling
and try to wash it clean.

But the blackness will not disappear . . .
then, one of them will slice it open,
to find the black knot clinging to the core.

The Good Return

(my great-great-grandfather's
trading ship—middle 1800s)

> All I know is he kept what he had by leaving it.
> —Debora Greger

My face is whittled by sunlight, the same harsh light
that turns even this New England water turquoise—
as if spilled through a funnel, a child's beach sieve,
the same brittle flood of glare that somewhere else takes

the color from the fields, draining the corn of its green,
pushing it into forgetfulness, to harvest, toward the shade
of dust.

Right before a storm the steep waves run in bunches
toward the beach,
and if I close my eyes I can still see the
strange shapes of maps . . .
imagine thrusting my arm
into one of the large porcelain jars lining the hold.

I can hold onto a memory as the captain keeps land
in perspective—waiting
for it to rise up real, a mountain again
at the edge of vision.

You can keep someone where you left her if you don't return . . .
in your mind she will remain in the house, walking it
like a nomad from window to window watching the water move
away from the shore.

Smell the thick whale oil burning.
A thin tail of smoke, thin as an animal trail hangs

in the inward reflection of a black window.
Land and water meeting without silhouette.

You could travel forever to get away—
keeping things you wanted out there.
You learned to enjoy the wanting, the waiting.
Remember the way the spoons were so thin, the family spoons,
silver—the details of trade, the things that were supposed to
   make you proud.

The footstep back, the black polished boots,
the heavy wood sea chest slowly lowering onto the deck—
Her desire landlocked in her breast,
still, in the rope bed,

strong as the smell of paint.

Venice, Widow in a Gondola 1891
for David

There is a thin line of shore in the distance
which holds a few indistinguishable buildings.
She sits in the cabin of the gondola, turned
to the back window and gripping with one hand a black hood,
making a fist, gathering the cloth under her chin.
She is a young woman and her other hand lightly
touches the window ledge.
Behind her is another window—
which leads the eye
to the white murky water.

Perhaps this is a ride in late afternoon,
self-indulgent or impulsive. She is waiting—
just waiting
the way she used to
for his figure to disappear in the haze,
down the street,
a dot with a newspaper tucked under his arm,
carrying the day's events—
growing smaller.

Safe House: Brandon, Vermont

(thinking of the underground railroad)

for W.P.

I hear someone digging in the basement,
a shovel raking up the last bit of gravel in a newly finished room.
Nervous laughter travels the pipes, whispers like a mouse
mapping a way to the stove.

The house down the road once belonged to a doctor
and the bedroom door is still tattooed with antique locks.
His wife was mad, the maid brought her supper on a tray
while the sunlight sulked through the room,
everything in too fine a focus.
Now, her ghost travels the perimeter of that darkened room—
a defused light.

The white house at the top of the hill has a room between floors,
a room totally undetectable from the outside,
from the inside, a place undetectable to the numb mind
of the man who searches. . . .
But this house has an extra room too—
a room in the basement behind a brick wall.
One has to crawl through some fake cupboards to get inside.

I found a black doll head there, under one of the plank beds.
And I know when I am not alone.
There is a soft knock on the dark window upstairs in the
    kitchen,
a lantern in town swings,
flashes on and off.
This is escape, migration, hidden progress—the north.

This is the northern kingdom, spring—the land of black mud.
Anxious horses side-step near the fence,
our faces
all dark in the unlit kitchen, we laugh, whisper
like swimmers drifting naked in the night.

A lilac branch snaps back, hits someone in the face,
dogs bark far off, there is smoke, the smell of cows—
and the mountains on all sides,
a cold that refuses to lift.

Self-Portrait with a Camellia Branch

Paula Modersohn-Becker, a painter,
lived and worked in the artist colony
in Worpswede, Germany. She died in 1907
at the age of 31, from complications
following childbirth.

The moors stretch out beyond the dull pane of the window,
they are a *delicious* brown; the water which moves slowly
through the canals is a dark *asphalt* black and the pine
and birch trees
possess qualities that make me see them as men and women.

I have cried a lot in my first year of marriage . . .
I feel as lonely as I did in childhood . . .
But here in my studio, turpentine lies in tin cups
like mercury waiting to be mixed. I slice some lemons,
my hands are raw and sting.
I am hungry.
I am a hungry woman.
I suck on a lemon quarter. I have a life here
surrounded by all this rotting fruit. The room smells sweet.
Still life.

There are things I want you to see—
the goosegirl with her sullen face—a barn against an evening
sky—an old woman hunched over holding a handkerchief—
the peat cutters in the field, the strain travels the length
of their hoes—the head and shoulders of a woman who has
   worked.

The sky is like milk, opaque,
and the sun burns behind it. The edges

of the landscape blur with the distance,
blue, like the glimpse from a carriage window.
The scene is like a charcoal drawing smudged.

It will snow tonight, even though it is spring,
*and through the sweet web of moonlight and delicate
snowy ether* that will surround me, I will paint myself
while I am solid and standing
in front of the mirror, holding a camellia branch.

I will paint myself over and over,
again and again until death takes the mirror away.

And this I say aloud,

And death, like the hills, rises up
dark and gray and sudden
from the flat promising fields.

The Prayer

> *It is my main concern to go beyond what I know and what I can know.*
>
> —Eva Hesse

There's a woman in this house who doesn't love herself
and her hands go so directly to the chicken,
to ripping it apart, that the feathers curl
on the floor like wood chips.

Before she even lights the oven, before
she curls her hair
she is outside walking a fallen field
between the rows where the smouldering fish
buried ages ago still flap slightly for air.

Someone is playing the spoons poorly in the distance
and the country air is heavy and restless.
This one day of foolish warmth, false spring as some call it,
brings back memories like the unfocused eye
slinging along the lights from an ongoing train window;
the lace along a neckline
makes way for

a young Amish woman in a white nightgown
scraping her fingernail at the peeling paint
of her bedroom window.
One woman loses her fingers in a printing press
and others dream of losing their teeth.

Where the barn swallows swim at dusk,
the hut that was the church
has been boarded up.

The Viaduct

for Tim

> *The only possible proof of the existence of water,*
> *the only convincing and intimately true proof, is thirst.*
> —Franz Von Baader

As children we wondered what was caught
on the river floor, what objects had drowned
and were pinned to the foundation of each arch.
It was a game. Birds flew out
from trees on either shore; we watched them
scatter like script across a page.

The sound there is always the same,
the rush of water, the wind moving across the railroad ties,
a weighty breath blowing over a bottle.
It seems that love is like the viaduct—
it is where we get caught . . .
and the train moves overhead in the dark.
The trestle shaking under its weight and speed.

I woke to the sound of the rain starting,
like a blind unraveling at the window,
at the end of the room.

Three

*To love purely is to consent to distance,
it is to adore the distance between ourselves
and that which we love.*
—Simone Weil

My Father

My father looks for his brother in heaven,
as if it were as simple as going from pub
to pub to find his face bent over a copper bar.
They are bachelors there—so they walk alone.
My mother thinks of my father as remarried,
living in one of those old European cities under bells
as she undoes a lettuce heart under running water.

And my father looks for my uncle
the way he did years ago in the park after a rain.
They were young and my father had just felt a girl's breast
for the first time.
Pink blossoms covered the black path—
and steam rose from the mud of the overturned tulip beds.
And my father looked for his brother not to boast,
but to tell how it felt as he let go.

Late August

A woman is like an elephant,
she never forgets what she sees.
So tell me something that will lead to a promise,
a statement as solid as a twig—that can later
be broken over my knee for a spring fire.
The dry wood could
spit back.

I yell into the wind
and my voice calling the dog
disappears—moves past me in the wrong direction.
It is early morning and the mist is pitched
in the shallow areas of the field.
The red dog weaves back and forth
on the exhausted land
in front of the house.

The yard is littered with brown horse-chestnut leaves.
Everything is a different color from before—
the small out-buildings are soaked wood,
the tree trunks black.
I just keep calling her in—
she stops for a moment in her tracks, and tips
her red head and continues on, away—down the cattle trail.

If this were a black-and-white photograph
someone would color my nightgown with photographic tints
as if it were the 1940s . . . the grass should be green,
the stones of the house, gray.

Equivalent

for JoEllen Kwiatek

There is nothing equivalent to the clouds—
summer clouds, long and thin like frayed rope
above the dark lake. Not even the bottom bed
of Lake George, that gradual soft mud slope down.
And you take pleasure in remembering yourself
in the different places of the past.

The mind returns to the past,
like a deer that moves gracefully in front
of the car like a premonition, only to re-enter the woods
as a shaft of light. It is summer and in the heat,
the denseness of failing light,
the house becomes invisible.

If you were to leave now,
it would be easy to drive down the two-lane highway
that pulls through the fields, then wait
to pull out behind the truck piled with wood cages
for white birds.

But you remain alone, preferring to think of the past,
the lake frozen under your feet, the white line
that formed itself around the lake, the culmination
of thousands of trees stripped of bark
across the middle of their trunks:
see, the browsing line; in winter the deer come out at night
and walk across the frozen lake to feed on the trees
at the edge of the shore

And you think of their ease,
to feed as animals do, on leaves and grass.
There is nothing more beautiful.

It has to do with comparison, speed and time,
clouds above the rupture of orange light, blue and gray,
slow moving as cattle grazing.

Translation
for Laura

Riding home on my bicycle I pass an old man
standing beside a bonfire—
It is the end of summer and his house is surrounded by
 cornfields;
along the hem of the fields small blue flowers bloom,
and from a distance the blue-green is heavy, like a child's
drawing with waxy crayons.

Going by the school I hear the students on the second floor,
the music sulking out of the huge open windows,
the light falling in chunks like ice onto the grass
from the louvered panes.
The sax and French horn.

The houses are spread out here, so I am watched for a long time,
pulling one foot up, then pushing the other down,
then the other up—standing in the saddle to make the hills.
When I ride at night like this, just before darkness has fallen,
I think of my mother, the past and when the days
were like flowers clipped at dusk
by her quick hands.

The Cedar Canoe

It is the end of the season.
And driving home back roads
past fields with stubble bright as spring,
flocks of small birds crisscross
like schools of fish through panels of light. I can feel
the temperature change like a swimmer passing over
channels that feed the lake.

The apples are ripe. The mill has started
filling jugs with cider. At night,
the workers drink beer in the orchard, muffling their laughter.
Children bang stones down on rolls of caps and lean
with the ladders against the shacks.

It is dark in the bedroom and the moon spreads
shadows of leaves across the ceiling, an underwater scene.
You lie with your back to me; I turn to look at the back of your
   head.
It is as if we are the couple on the motorcycle,
we nod, and point toward the landscape and yell
necessary directions.

I put my arms around your waist.
I am thinking of your mother's cedar canoe. You are in front
of me pointing out over the reservoir. Two loons disappear
and resurface across the lake.
Water slowly seeps into the cedar, the paddles push
through the water.
I can hear the noise we make even when we move.

Sunday Morning

The light seems to come from the tiger lilies
on the hill above the barn. It is a direct light with contrast.
And when one wakes on a day such as this,
I actually think of gravity—the idea of it,
the way my foot is pulled
toward the wood floor under the bed,
the manner in which things are thrown in the air—
the baby,
the ball—and the man asleep beside me,
his face so taut as he curls on the bed.

The heart seems like a stall,
empty and wood. A shaft of floral light enters
through a broken pane.

Think of the heart breaking,
as if it were a string on a perfectly tuned violin—
or that the breaking is really a slow crumble,
a small stall where the fire starts,
which burns and then levels the whole barn
in an early morning fire.

Then, if you believe in God, imagine the voice,
the tiger lilies, flames burning in the rut next to the road,
the kind of fire that is left
to burn itself out. . . .
Imagine the barn where the hands of tobacco
hang upside down to dry

and move in a breeze—a slight wind that slips
through the slats of the barn . . .

the sound is thin and light,
as if something were being lifted.

Crossing

The harsh light falls in a bright square
on the floor, it falls like a thick trapdoor on a hinge—
suddenly in the morning like a hole with stairs underneath,
a way out.

Or the light falls heavily like cold water,
it stumbles like water that has just rolled back
to being liquid. You can be sure it's forgotten being a floor,
solid, a bridge to reach the opposite shore.

Just beyond the house
the falls are honey-combed with ice, pock-marked and jagged
and bright. The silver birches on the opposite shore are real
but also what I dream of.

So here, I am constantly watching the falls.
I will hear water rushing again
for a long time to come.
While light moves in puddles over the bare trees.

This is when we all dream—
just before we wake.
I walk out of the house and in front where the road
should be is a river—
it is bright, too bright to look toward.
The rapids are so reflective I have to squint, cover one eye.

My lover says,
look and there on the opposite side of the river
birches glitter—

the sunlight forms huge columns
and it is so beautiful that we have to cross.
And he tells me not to worry, that the water isn't deep.

The Awakening

> *There is no casino like the heart's.*
> —David St. John

The train moves through the fields like an afterthought,
or a barge moaning, heavy with coal as the horses pull it along
on the iron water of the canal.
The whistle is different in the rain—

as thunderclouds move over the houses
like huge boats above schools of fish.
I hear my sister from my guest room let out a light cry,
as if in disbelief while making love,
like the sound a thread would make going through the eye
of a needle.
And it sounded so much like my own voice
coming through the wall.

You are gone now, and I think of your absence
as if you were a plant out of season—it just doesn't bloom
    anymore.
I remember how you climbed the stairs
after you had been driving for days,
not as if you went up and down the coast at the change of each
    season
but as if you were a waiter
who had just finished work down the street,
with tips in his pockets and crabmeat on his breath,
leaning down, over me, to kiss me
awake.

The Lake
for Fred

The water is the color of Chinese green tea,
and thick, as I slide in. You are standing on the shore
looking past me. Behind you is the summer house.
Through encrusted screens comes the clatter
of silverware being washed in the tin tub.
Small children run quietly
in and out of the bushes at the side of the house.

I think back to this morning—
in the wet heat, we picked the blueberries
among the scuff of bushes lining the dirt road.

As I swim farther,
I can see the other small docks.
There are still a few lone figures
winding up lines, securing small boats.

My chin slides down into the water.
I am eye-level with the lake.
There are pines on the opposite shore.
You yell out; I cannot make out what you say.
You turn and walk into the house.
The screen door snaps shut.

It is dusk and everything has lost its color.
I hang in the water next to the diving platform.
The air is too cool to pull myself out
and onto the watersoaked wood.
Instead, I hang there, my legs drifting,
drifting away, underneath the dock.

The Contemporary Poetry Series

Edited by Paul Zimmer

Dannie Abse, *One-Legged on Ice*
Gerald Barrax, *An Audience of One*
Tony Connor, *New and Selected Poems*
Franz Douskey, *Rowing Across the Dark*
Lynn Emanuel, *Hotel Fiesta*
John Engels, *Vivaldi in Early Fall*
John Engels, *Weather-Fear: New and Selected Poems, 1958–1982*
Brendan Galvin, *Atlantic Flyway*
Brendan Galvin, *Winter Oysters*
Michael Heffernan, *The Cry of Oliver Hardy*
Michael Heffernan, *To the Wreakers of Havoc*
Conrad Hilberry, *The Moon Seen as a Slice of Pineapple*
X. J. Kennedy, *Cross Ties*
Caroline Knox, *The House Party*
Gary Margolis, *The Day We Still Stand Here*
Michael Pettit, *American Light*
Bin Ramke, *White Monkeys*
J. W. Rivers, *Proud and on My Feet*
Laurie Sheck, *Amaranth*
Myra Sklarew, *The Science of Goodbyes*
Marcia Southwick, *The Night Won't Save Anyone*
Mary Swander, *Succession*
Bruce Weigl, *The Monkey Wars*
Paul Zarzyski, *The Make-Up of Ice*

The Contemporary Poetry Series

Edited by Bin Ramke

J. T. Barbarese, *Under the Blue Moon*
Richard Cole, *The Glass Children*
Wayne Dodd, *Sometimes Music Rises*
Joseph Duemer, *Customs*
Karen Fish, *The Cedar Canoe*
Sydney Lea, *No Sign*
Gary Margolis, *Falling Awake*
Aleda Shirley, *Chinese Architecture*
Susan Stewart, *The Hive*
Terese Svoboda, *All Aberration*